"There are very few books of Love Text Messages on the market. Armand Del Tor's book is a definite winner amongst them with its genuine emotions, impressive depth, and beautiful English."

—Samantha Russell, KS

"I am impressed with Armand Del Tor's imagination! So many comparisons of Love with natural phenomena! In those messages you can feel his love bursting out of his heart with the full force of an erupting volcano!"

—Lucia Marquez, IL

"Powerful! Exciting! Romantic! And some are funny! I cannot believe love can be expressed in so many ways and in such short messages."

—William Macmillan, MA

"I enjoyed reading the book! Once you start with the first message, you want to read more and more. With all the gamma of emotions you feel, it seems like reading a brilliantly written novel."

—Irena Politkovskiy, NY

"A very useful book for couples, especially for those who cannot verbalize their emotions. I liked all the text messages, with the exception of the few in the Spicy Chapter, which were a little too spicy for me."

—Lloyd Harold, TX

"In every message you can feel the tender and caring heart."

—Abby Sinclair, MI

"Affectedly sentimental, just as true love is."

George Cruzan, AZ

"If all these messages have been sent to one person, then I am really jealous of that person!"

—Nancy Barrymore, CA

Lovely! Each message is charged with passion and love."

—Maya Schwarzkopf, NY

THE BOOK

OF LOVE TEXT MESSAGES

The Perfect Gift For All

ARMAND DEL TOR

FIRST EDITION

AMAC & PUBLISHING, INC.

VERONA   NEW JERSEY   USA

Published by
AMAC & Publishing, Inc.
28 Elk Road
Verona, NJ 07044

For Information address AMAC and Publishing, Inc.,
28 Elk Road, Verona, NJ, 07044-2501

ISBN-13: 978-0-9832028-0-6
Library of Congress Control Number: 2010919544

Cover and Interior design by
Kimberly Martin, Jera Publishing, LLC

Printed In the United States of America by
Lightning Source Inc. (US)

First Edition

10 9 8 7 6 5 4 3 2 1

For the love of my life and the source of my constant inspiration – my family.

Two souls with but a single thought,
Two hearts that beat as one.
— Friedrich Halm

Whenever you have truth it must be
given with love, or the message and the
messenger will be rejected.
— Mahatma Gandhi

ACKNOWLEDGMENTS

I want to thank AMAC & Publishing, Inc. and my editor Mariam Swayze for all the invaluable advice and thoroughness.

I thank Jera Publishing and Kimberly Martin for the design of the book.

Many thanks to all, who kindly agreed to read the manuscript, gave recommendations, and shared their thoughts and impressions.

I want to thank my wife for being who she is, for all the support she has provided, for all the love she has given to me throughout the 21 years we are together, and for her consent to share the messages addressed to her with the world.

I thank my daughter and son for being the wonderful kids they are, for all their love, hugs and kisses.

I also want to thank all my friends and relatives who are always with us in good times and in bad times, ready to help and give important advice.

And finally I thank everyone who encouraged me to publish this Book of Love Messages.

Armand Del Tor

FOREWORD

Dear Reader,

I will consider my mission complete if, by reading this book, just only two hearts rejoin, just one family survives, and just one divorce is avoided.

In this high-paced and economically unstable world, with longer work hours, longer commute, and constant stress, we do not find time to communicate enough with our loved ones. Little or no communication leads to distantiating from each other, losing the strong emotional ties we once had. This, in its turn, leads to indifference, living together like strangers, then separation or divorce.

Writing letters has been a wonderful way of expressing love for many centuries. But the era of writing letters is long gone. Modern technology and lifestyle have made that wonderful way of communication obsolete.

Email and text messages have replaced them.

How many of us have ever thought to use them on a regular basis to express true love and togetherness? Of course, most couples will end their text messages with a short 'Love you'. But that's the extent of expressing love throughout the day in today's busy life.

You could make your relationship stronger by giving a little thought and spending only five minutes just once a week (of course the more the better) and 'texting' your emotions, love, and caring in so many different ways.

Text messages could help restore your relations quickly after arguments, 'fights' and misunderstanding. Find the courage to make the first step. Depending on the situation, send a message of love, forgiveness, apology, understanding, and acceptance. Never put aside the reconciliation for a later time. Life is short. We never know when and where it ends. Try to give all the warmth of your heart to your loved one now.

No matter how busy you are, no matter where you are, you can always find those few minutes for the most important person of your life.

The book you are reading contains more than three hundred text messages expressing a wealth of emotions. Love dominates in all of them.

This is a book of genuine love and all messages are inspired by the only woman in my life.

I am ready to share my thoughts and emotions with the world. I hope they will inspire many people to look at their intimate lives more attentively, find the reasons for their unsettling feeling of loneliness while still living with the person they loved once, and try to revive it. For those who are in love, this book could serve as a guide to keep it burning with inextinguishable flames for their lifetime…

I am sure most of the messages will make a 'connection' in your heart. Text them to your beloved half. Gradually you'll find your own thoughts and words to express LOVE, the strongest of all the God-given feelings.

With Love,

Armand Del Tor

CONTENTS

EXPRESS YOUR LOVE

My Love to you is like thirst in the desert…
with not a single drop of water… nothing but the
thought of thirst… I Love You!

I was trying to figure out how my love, the size of
the universe, can fit into my heart, the size of my fist…
and I found the answer… my love constantly flows
from my heart to you day and night without stopping…
I love you eternally…

… A valley of flowers… a canyon of diamonds…
an ocean of love… all to you… from my heart…
I Love you!!!!!!!!!!!!

The Queen of my Heart! Your splendid grace and
majestic beauty make me ecstatic and feel like a king!
I embrace you and give you a royal kiss…

My love! My soul is so intertwined with yours that
I can feel the slightest fluctuations of your mood and
attitude… and when you are sad or edgy, so am I,
and when you are 'smiley' and happy, so am I…
Love you always… wishing you lots of smiles…

If I were a yoga master and was capable of stopping
my heart temporarily, even then I would not be able
to stop your resonating heartbeat in me…
I love you with every beat of your heart…

I don't eat sugar, because I have the sweetest woman
in the world… I don't go to the art galleries, because I
have my own masterpiece at home… I don't watch the
stars in the sky, because I have a shining star right next
to me… I have YOU!… I love you!

My love seems to be in constant race… with the rushing
time… It wants to leave unfading marks of happiness on
your face and in your heart to fight all the wrinkles that
time is trying to leave… I love you…

My love... the deep brown of your eyes is haunting me... sending electrocuting impulses halting my breath... and making me wish for more... to feel the constant desire to be choked by your love... I love you...

Take my hand and feel my pulse... it throbs in unison with your heartbeat... Can you feel it, my LOVE?

All these days I was missing the opportunity to send you my messages of love... affection... desire... unity... devotion... Today I am sending all that in a bundle... wrapped in pink, and a red rose attached... as a symbol of my loving heart...

I love you...

Thank you baby. Your love to me is the biggest gift of my life! God bless our Love!

(In response to Happy Birthday message from her).

My adorable! Life is so short to let me give
you all my Love... Yours in eternity!

My sunshine! I just felt your warmth
spreading through me... I LOVE YOU too!

I heard your voice! So sweet and so dear!
My soul is reaching you to feel the voice of your heart...
Love Forever!

My Destiny! My Love! In true love there are no favors...
only the desire to make your other half happy... and it
should come from the bottom of your heart...

My love and my air... I still feel your heartbeat when we
were dancing on the floor and... in the bed... Let the
dance of our souls be an eternal symbol of togetherness
and mutual devotion... Love you forever!

My love! I am not calling because I know it's hard
for you to talk. My thoughts and my heart are always
with you... Just feel my hug, and my gentle kiss and
you'll feel better... I love you very much...

My love and passion! Your image always accompanies
me... day and night... and makes me feel you next to
me... loving and caring... Love you 24/7 ...!

My love, the only way you find peace inside is to love
me as strongly as I love you. I kiss you everywhere...

You are My love! And My desire! But love always comes
first! Take my heart and keep it to feel its everlasting
wish to live and die for you... I love you!

My radiant love!! Your bright image keeps
me going despite any pain and discomfort...
Love you now and forever...

My love! I have this inexplicable feeling of incompleteness when we are apart. And nothing can replace that feeling except your soothing words of love and devotion... I love you... you are my life...

My marvelous! I can still taste your morning kiss... so sweet and so desirable... I kiss you back with all the passion of my heart! I Love you baby!

My love! I feel as if I have not seen you a very-very long time... My heart achingly wants to reach you and hug you both tenderly and passionately... I love you! I miss you!

As the workday approaches its end, so does my patience... so many hours without your presence is torture... love you very much!

My love! I wish I had more time to express all the tremendous love and tenderness I feel for you... For now – just close your eyes and feel my loving kiss on your lips...

My love! I have this inexplicable feeling of emptiness without you at home... even though I am keeping myself extremely busy...

I have no life without you... How can I live without oxygen? Give me breath... I love you!

I feel better after your message... But nothing cures me better than your lovely voice when we are apart...

My eternal love! If my heart knew how to beat as long as yours will, it would... to give all the love until the last beat, to make you feel loved till the end... and if doesn't, it will send love to you from heaven...

My love! I want my heart to connect to yours, so you feel
that my love pours into you every second, so that you do
not have the chance to forget about your love even for a
moment... I Love you non-stop!

My day is meaningful only if I feel your love, even from
the distance separating us... and I want you to feel my
love the same way... I miss you my LOVE!

My only one! Your lovely smile in the photo on my desk
is like a balm for my tired eyes... and soul...
I love you dearly...

My life! I am missing you so much... thank God it's
Friday and I'll embrace you soon and enjoy the
weekend with you... I love you forever!

My love and my life! Your stunning beauty is inspiring,
your loving and caring attitude – unforgettable...
I press my lips against your ear and whisper
over and over – I love you...

My and mine! Fridays are especially hard to endure at work as my heartbeat accelerates from early morning and my eyes reject to see anything in anticipation of seeing your lovely face and pressing you firmly to my chest and feeling you…

My love! Your dazzling beauty and both your currently reserved and yet-to-be-revealed limitless love accompany me day and night… Open up more… Give all you have in your heart as I give mine… I love you!

My love! Today my heart has this unclear feeling of alarm and discomfort… and this unstoppable desire to hold you in my arms and put my head on your shoulder and absorb your warmth and tenderness… I love you…

My happiness! I still enjoy the memories of the wonderful moments from yesterday, and I am looking forward to many happy returns of those moments of love, intimacy, understanding and mutuality… My heart always beats for you… I love you…

My life! Your every emotion is part of me… I smile when you are happy; I suffer when you are sad or ill… I would give the entire world to make you happy all the time… I love you eternally…

My love! My heart and my soul are reaching you to give you all the powers of love and eternal unity. Embrace them and feel how much I love you…

My Sweetheart! When separated by distance, I miss you all the time, feeling only one half of me, and it makes me feel so incomplete… I love you and I'm looking forward to gaining my completeness…

Guess – Who is the one and the only one?... Who is the best and the very best?... Who is the Sun and the hottest Sun? Who is the Beauty and the unchallenged Beauty…

… … …

It's my lovely (her name goes here)!!! I love you!

My only joy in the orb! I love you and cherish
each and every smile of yours, each and every
kiss of yours... Now go back to the very beginning
of the message and write down the first letters of all
the six words of my greeting... then close your eyes
and remember us enjoying it and each other the
whole day on Saturday...
I love you...

My loving heart is yours... my loving thoughts
are with you... my loving care is for you...
my firm and loving grasp is to comfort you...
I am totally and irrevocably yours...
I love you!

From the day that we met, you have been
my one and only one, you are and you will be...
as long as God defines eternity...
I love you!

Make a wish... now count to 5... now imagine it came
true!.. Make a second wish... Count to 3... Imagine it
came true too... and again... make a wish... count 1...
imagine it came true too! Now let me tell you... I don't
know what you wished for... As for me... No matter
how many times I try to make a wish... I can't... Because
my only wish in life has come true a long time ago...
I have YOU!.!.!..!...! I love you!

It's time to put an end... to the pretense... that I love
you... I don't... Because the word 'love' is too short, too
plain, too often used by many others... to express the
unique, overwhelming, and over-embracing gamma of
my feelings to you... I came up with a new word...
I 'IdolAdoroLovExaltoVeneratoCrushoGlorify' you!!!

My unforgettable! Your scent, your smile,
your movement, your kiss, your warmth,
your touch... are with me all the time... I
IdolAdoroLovExaltoVenerateoCrushoGlorify you!

We have been out of touch for 7 hours… seems like 7 years to me… hence my 7 wishes… Hear you at least every 7 hours, see you every 7 minutes, kiss you every 7 seconds, touch you every 7 milliseconds, hug you every 7 microseconds, hold you every 7 nanoseconds… and feel you every 7 picoseconds… I Love You!

Tonight I woke up from my own snoring… but then I was wondering why I still heard the snoring being awake… Then I realized it was now your snoring… I closed my eyes and thought about it as the most pleasant music I have ever heard… I fell back to sleep very quickly… I love you…

I am all wired up because of the unexpected volume of work today. Only your soothing image in my mind and heart is helping me go through the day… I love you…

Look into your eyes… in the mirror… Then look into my
eyes… in your mind… What you will see in both cases is
expectation from the other… for a smile… for a huge
hug… for a long and passionate kiss… and for hearing
the magic of the three words – I Love You!... Right now
I did all four… I smiled… then closed my eyes and
imagined myself in your warm embrace, kissing you
passionately… and me whispering to you –
I Love You… and waiting for your whisper…

Today I did not see you and did not kiss you before
leaving to work, and you did not respond to my wish to
have a great day, as you did not hear my wish because
of the running water… and I was so upset… until you
called… When I hear you – I survive… When I see you –
I breathe… When I kiss you – I live… I love you!

… In our favorite song it says 'You are my joy and
you are my sorrow'. There is some truth in it. But
I would prefer to say 'You are my joy… and you
are my happiness…'. I love you!

My lovely beauty! I have this constant head-spinning
sensation every day when I am away from you. It
disappears the moment I hug you... and then it turns
into heart-spinning... which doesn't stop even when
I am asleep... So my life is a constant love-induced
spinning cycle: head-heart-head-heart...
I love you in a never-ending cycle...

When it's silent, I listen to your heart... When there
is noise around, I look into your eyes... When I am close
to you, I smell your scent... When I am far from you,
I see your silhouette... And I feel the 'togetherness' –
in joy and depression, in love and anger, in despair
and hope... I love you...

My love. I hope my late message will find
you in a happy Friday mood with a big smile on
your face and a lot of love in your heart, just as much
as is always reserved for you in my heart...
I LOVE YOU!

Knock-knock! It's me! The one and only one!
Your only one, to be more precise! The one who has
put his heart and soul and body into one bundle and
given to his one and only one... to his lovely
(Her Name or Nickname Here)...
I love you baby...

As my busy day comes to its end, so does my
patience... With this busy schedule, I was angry
that I couldn't find a moment until now to send
my Love to you... I miss you...

From sunrise to sunset... and then from
sunset to sunrise... my heart beats for you...
sometimes calmly... but mostly in rapid succession...
in powerful throbs... trying to send all the passion
it has... in burning waves... to reach you...
and make your heart melt in the sweet delight
of choking from love... I love you...

Why do people like Fridays? Most people like it because they will be off from work the next two days. But I like Fridays, because they hold more promise than the other days... promise of undivided time with you... promise of your physical presence near me... the promise of sharing chores, thoughts, space, auras, silence... everything... together... I love you Monday through Friday 24 hours a day, and Saturday and Sunday – 48 hours with no interruptions...

Hello darling, and welcome to my embrace... I am here to hug you at all times... Make sure to use the opportunity to feel loved as often as you can... because... although I am here for you for a lifetime, our lifetime itself is expiring with each second... I love you...

If the meeting were to last a half hour more, I would have missed the chance to send my message of love and kisses to you today... Luckily it just ended... And I am typing in a hurry to tell that you are always in my heart and mind... I love you...

When I am not around I am just one phone call away…
But whether I am around or one phone call away…
I am with you always… with my endless love
and my heart under your feet…
I love you…

My dreamy eyes see only one picture…
My sensitive hearing distinguishes only one tune…
My smelling receptors catch only one smell…
your picture… your melody… your smell…
I love you…

This was a Thursday, which felt like Monday…
But the bright side of it is… that tomorrow IS Friday…
only a day away from 'Our Friday Night'…
when, although tired from the work-week
'baggage', we will feel the exaltation of being
inseparably close to embrace and kiss each other
any time we like the next two days…
I love you…

No bouquet will be able to convey all my love, all my
feelings to you... and yet, I put part of me in each
bouquet, for you to feel the warmth and the
tenderness... the strength and the passion... of my
love... to accompany you the next 80 years... I love
you...

Although I enjoyed the 'dad and son' evening very
much, it left a feeling of incompleteness... the short
encounter with you in the morning was not enough for
me to get rid of that feeling throughout the day... I need
you more... I need you always... I

love you...

Commute... Work... Chores... The cold... But I look at
all that positively... since there is always the realization
that along with all that comes the wonderful time with
you... I love you...

The Holiday Season is wonderful... because we have several extra days in the month to be together all day long... I am looking forward to those days... with the tingling expectation of your warm breath, charming smile, your kisses and hugs... I love you...

The only time I stop thinking of you is when I am deep asleep, because when I am deep asleep I see you in my dream... I love you...

I am one of the endangered species... and not because of air and water pollution or lack of food... I just need your constant presence... Every minute away from you shortens my life as much... I love you...

I just remembered the wonderful lines from Beatles... 'Limitless undying love which shines around me like a million suns, it calls me on and on, across the universe'... I love you baby...

I got lost in the maze of my feelings… Do I love you as my wife? Do I love you as my friend? Do I love you as my lover? All answers are YES, but I don't know which one prevails… I love you…

My love! As the work day goes by, so does a part of my life without seeing you… without feeling your warmth… and that's why I always try to fill this gap with kisses and hugs of love and tenderness… I miss you… I love you…

*

Send this in three messages with one minute intervals:

I fell… … ..

… desperately and irreversibly in love with you… 20 years ago…

… the fall still continues… deeper and deeper… and my heart screams… I LOVE YOU!!!

And continue on the next day:

… so … when I fell, I felt extremely dizzy, disoriented and… extremely happy… as one feels after the right dose of a drug… and I still feel the same now… drugged with my love to you… forever!

EXPRESS YOUR LOVE VIVIDLY

Where is Heaven? Is it in the North? Or is it in the
South? Or maybe in the West? Or in the East? Is it in the
skies? Or is it on the earth? If you chose any of those,
you are wrong... as Heaven is in the deep of your eyes...
in the melody of your voice... in the track of your
footprint... in the hint of your scent... in the imprint of
your touch... YOU are Heaven..! I love you...

My Fairy! I am constantly mesmerized by your unfading
magic and charm... and I am determined to stay in that
state forever... even in afterlife... I love you...

Today I talked to an angel and asked to come to
you tonight to protect your sleep... But she said an
angel cannot protect the sleep of another angel... So all
I can offer you – is to take my loving heart with you into
your dreams to feel its warmth and lulling serenity to
keep you in the world of Morpheus longer...
I love you my Angel...

I just discovered… I have left my remote key at home.
Now I have to wait until I am back… to unlock your
heart… and listen to its waves of love… bouncing
against the rocks of my soul… I love you…

There is a legend that the heart was initially
created round… then God changed it into a 'heart'-
shape, so that one half be the self, and the other –
the God-given Love, and that they are together
until the heart stops… I love you… feeling
you inside me with every heartbeat…

Remember the legend about the heart?
That legend does not say which half is the self,
and which half is its love… I think you are the left
half of my heart, as the left half delivers the
oxygenated blood to all parts of the body
keeping it alive… I love you!

⬯⬯⬯

Once upon a time… when God had not yet created anything, there was nothing… except God's love… which he later gave to each of his creations… My love for you was born in those days to last as long as God completes the cycle… turning everything into nothing… Until then… I love you…

⬯⬯⬯

Good afternoon Mrs. (Her Last Name Here). On this (Today's Day)th day of (Month), of the year (Year), your dear husband & lover and life-long friend, Mr. (Your Last Name Here), has extended you his tender and passionate feelings of limitless love, complete devotion, absolute exaltation, veneration and glorification. Please RSVP upon receipt of this heart-warming announcement to accept all the above-mentioned feelings in their entirety, and to confirm the mutuality of the same on your behalf. Duly signed and dated under oath by Mr. (Your Last Name Here) in the office of Love&Passion Affairs. Addendum: The feelings expressed by the signer have no limitations and no expiration date.

⬯⬯⬯

Is there life on Mars? Sure there is! And there is life on all planets… Because my love to you is all over the universe… So where there is love, there is life… I love you cosmically!

A fistful of diamonds, a handful of dark red roses,
and a 'heartful' of love are my wishes to you today…
and don't forget that the third wish is not just a wish…
It's a fact of a lifetime… My lifetime…
I love you always and forever…

If I had a magic wand, I would do only one thing…
Make a miniature clone of you the size of a small doll,
and carry it with me always and everywhere…
to feel your presence… to talk to you when I want…
to kiss you when I want… and to tell you all the
time how much I love you…

Attention: This message is very important and has been
routed from (Her First Probable Location) to
(Her Second Probable Location). If the addressee is not
in (Her Second Location), it will be available in
(Her First Location) again…

This is to announce the opening of heart-to-heart direct
communication of Love from the sender to the recipient
with a mandatory immediate cardiac response.
A package of 1001 kisses to all sensitive areas of the
recipient is attached…

My heart is in flames… of love… but I don't need a fire extinguisher… I want it to burn in blinding glow to light your way to my heart… I love you…

Have you heard about anyone who would like to spend all his life in jail? Let me introduce probably the only one in the world who does… It's me… I was sentenced to life imprisonment the moment I met you… and then was put in jail 2 years later… jail of your astounding charm and unparalleled beauty… and I will be in jail the rest of my life tying chains of love around you… to hold you in the same cell with me forever… I love you in jail…

If I caught the GoldFish I would ask it
to grant these three wishes:

1. Let my wife be young and healthy forever

2. Let my kids be young and healthy forever

3. Let me see that it works…

I love you…

Do you know who invented the wheel? I do not know either... And nobody does. But unlike the majority, who think it was invented to make the movement from one place to another quicker, I think it was invented in an attempt to create something to rotate forever as a symbol of true and endless love... I love you in the endless motion of the wheel...

To be or not to be in Heaven without love...
My answer is not to be... If I cannot have you in Heaven, than it's not Heaven at all... I love you...

My heartbeat counts in 2s... whereas my love counts in millions... representing all the heartbeats of my life since I met you... each and every one of them empowered by you... each and every one of them for you... I love you with each and every heartbeat...

I feel like I am floating... on turbulent waves... and with each up I hear your name and with each down I hear your laugh... I love you with every up and down...

I am your light bulb... waiting for you to turn on the switch... to brighten the dark... to glow for you... to illuminate any path you step on... I love you...

The more I live, the more I love you... and I can't stop wondering, how that big a love can get even bigger... it's probably because my love is like being in the never-ending Universe... the further it travels, the more it has to cover... I love you...

My life! I am blinded by the light emanating from you... and want to spend the rest of my life in that sweet blindness... I love you...

My Love! I wish there was a way to make a network connection between you and me like computers, so that we always stay tuned to each other and feel each other every single nanosecond without interruption... I love you baby!

My love! My internal thermometer indicates high mid 100s in the heart area... My internal barometer indicates high blood pressure in the arteries... My internal speedometer indicates extreme acceleration of heartbeat... All because my internal sensor indicates elevated levels of love and desire... I love you...

My love! Today my heart feels like a helicopter caught in a whirlwind... except that the helicopter is revving in an attempt to get out of the whirlwind, whereas my heart is revving to stay in the whirlwind... because it's the whirlwind of my love to you... I love you in the storming whirlwind...

Go to {Yourname Here}@Heart.Wait and enter your password... It should be 4 characters long, start with the capital letter L, and be a true expression of your feeling. When your password is accepted, you will be redirected to the wonderful site of {Yourname Here}@Love.Big... I love you in cyberspace...

☙ EXPRESS AFFLICTION TOO... ❧

When upset – remember that I am here to cheer you
up… When angry or mad – remember that I am here
to take your rage… When you are in denial of your own
love – remember that I still love… as We are meant to
be in love together until the end of the world…
I love you…

My love! My heart and mind are aching…
seeking cure in your smile, gentle kisses, and warmth…
lovingly yours…

My love. All is because of my love! But I cannot love you
less. I am crazy about you!

My love! Make sure to keep each broken piece
of my heart… Each will continue radiating my
love to you forever…

My love, Life is short. Only Love must we give to each
other and to our kids… I pray for that… I love you…

My only way to survive is to be inspired by your love...
Give it to me incessantly to keep me alive...
with every breath I say – I love you...

My love! My heart feels lonely, my soul – vacant without
your presence and touch... I lovingly miss you...
and need you...

What can be greater than the universe?
My love to you and... my suffering!
Is your love to me really just an act?

Another day passes without a single word from my
beloved... another day of waiting for your heart to feel
my distant quest for love and mutuality... will I last long
like this?... oh I love you till I die...

When there is sadness in my eyes, look deeper in their
blue... and you will see my aching heart calling you to
love me the only way true love is meant to be –
unconditionally and purely... with no one else in
between... I love you until there is at least one
flower and one last breath to share...

If you talk to my heart it will tell you it's drained
and tired, and the only reason it does not stop is the
hope to feel your sincere love and complete devotion...
Don't make it stop... It beats for you... and loves you...

My love! I miss you so much! I send you all my tender
and passionate love! Feel it and love me more...
forever yours...

My Love! Have I crossed your mind or heart yet today?
Love you all the more!

My love, after a sleepless and rough night
I was longing for your soothing voice...

My Love and Beauty! My aching heart is always there for you! Just take it gently and caress it to feel it still beats only for you, and it will heal if your heart beats only for me! Embrace my LOVE and you'll feel it's the only thing that will never die, even when I'm gone... Yours forever... I Love you!!!

My life! Nothing seems real to me anymore... I feel my eternal love to you has made me blind... preventing me from seeing anything else but you... my tears are dropping from my blind eyes... and yet... I love you...

My love! It's always so unsettling when you are not home... it's a torture to be home and not to hear your lovely voice and not to see your beautiful face... All my other thoughts and all chores I am doing today are constantly interrupted by your image and the intolerable feeling of incompleteness... I miss you so much..!

My love! Saying I miss you is such an understatement for what I feel... I feel completely desolate... awfully incomplete... I need you... I love you...

If this was the last day of my life… I would wish you to forget me the moment I take my last breath… But as I hope it is not… I wish you to remember to love me… day and night… just the way I love you…

My Love! I regret so much that I had to spend so much time away from you yesterday… Today I have this nagging feeling of something incomplete, of something bitter… for the hours lost… And this feeling of missing you so much… I love you my beauty…

I want you to smile, I want you to rejoice, I want you to laugh… to make my aching mind and body heal… to never stop giving you all my love and passion… I love you…

Is love always blind? I think it is… except when it senses something wrong and 'opens its eyes' just to confirm itself despite the 'wrong' it sees… I love you blindly…

Is everything ok baby? I did not hear from you today and you did not answer/return my call… I feel like asking our son's question – Do you still love me? ☺

…No matter how hard you try to cool me down by not calling me at all (6 days in a row)… I will find the time and the desire to tell I love you…

This was a pretty silent week… and a week of some detachment from each other… But I hope my love was reaching you even through the silence… to make you feel better… I love you always…

∞LOVE AND NATURE∞

My love to you is like the magma in a volcano
turning into lava when bursting out of the crater...
unforgiving and powerful in its determination
to absorb you entirely... I love you...

∞

My love to you starts at the source of the river...
turning into a tumultuous current of an unstoppable
feeling flowing through the maze of emotions to the
estuary... to join the ocean... of your love...
I love you in the torrent...

∞

My love to you is overwhelming, out of any
boundaries, and uncontrollable... It's like a tsunami...
except it directs itself only to you... and crashes
only on you to cover you with an enormous
wave of passion and love...

The leaves have started falling… Soon everything will be
in color… The fall will once again demonstrate its
powerful and unparalleled beauty… Don't miss the
chance to look around… and enjoy… since every leaf
with its unique color is a gift from me to you…
to express the number of my vivid thoughts about you…
and all the wonderful shades of auras accompanying my
thoughts and feelings on their endless journey to you…
I love you in the leaves of the fall…

I want to be a flower… a flower in your hands. I want to
be a droplet of rain… a droplet of rain floating down
your face. I want to be a snowflake… a snowflake
melting on your lips. I want to be… just anything…
to touch you… to feel you… I love you…

No dense clouds can block the light of love, as its force
of penetration is the most powerful of all forces… I am
sending my love with the force of lightning… to you…
through the clouds… clearing the way for the sunshine
of my heart to reach you… I love you!

⚭

The hurricane season is approaching… both in the ocean and in my heart… So better be prepared for frequent storms of passion and whirlwinds of love… I love you!

⚭

You are my mayflower! You blossom even in the midst of winter! I feel your lovely aroma everywhere… I love you always!

⚭

My pearl! Your glitter intensifies more and more each day giving the joy of light to my eyes and the joy of happiness to my soul! I love you enormously!

⚭

My darling! Let this late message of love and devotion warm you up on this cold day and give you the feeling of comfort and peace… I love you!

⚭

My only desire! You and Only You can set the fire in me and make me crazy… with my own love to you…

My love. Yesterday, when looking at the stars on the night sky, I imagined you as one of them... except your shining is so close, so warm and so loving... in contrast to their distant and cold glow... I love you with the size of the sky and all of the stars combined...

My love! You are my heat when I am cold, you are my breeze when I am hot, you are my remedy when I am ailing... you are my everything... I love you!

My charming flower! No rose can compete with your grace, no edelweiss with your wonder, no carnation with your beauty... I love you!

If you try to see with my eyes, you'll see a big and shining sun with your smiling face on it! I love you with all the sunshine of my heart!

My tigress! I love you so much, that even your occasional roaring and grumbling seem like music to me... I love you, my creature of the jungle...

My love! Close your eyes and imagine the illumination of a giant lightning strike on the dark cloudy sky of the night…That's what I experience every time, when I think of you – blinding illumination followed by breathtaking thunder… and then… the desire to experience it again and again… I love you…

Honey! It's gorgeous outside. I hope you are taking breaks to get away from the office dust and enjoy the sun… which will remind you that my heart radiates even more warmth to you than any burning star in the universe! I LOVE YOU!

My adorable! My cloudy Sunshine! Break through those clouds with your glowing beams and spread your heat upon me…to match the heat of my inextinguishable love to you…

…another rainy gloomy day… with my bright thoughts about you… I love you!

My love to you is like a hurricane, except it doesn't ruin.

When it's cloudy dark and drizzly dull, your smiling face makes my day bright! I Love you my shining sun...

The spring of my life and soul! Unlike the snow and the cold, on the first day of spring, you make me feel as if I'm in flowers and warmth all year round... I love you... kissing you with my hot summer kisses...

My love-bird! I miss your voice, as sweet as the morning chirps, your touch as gentle as that of a feather, the sensual lips like the beak of the feeding mother-bird... I love you...

My love! The magnitude of my love for you can only be compared to the endless universe... its intensity – to the sun's huge flares... I am burning with love... from love...

The Love of my life... and the fire of my love! I send you the flames of my burning heart to make you feel warm on this unusually cold spring day and to fill you with my inextinguishable love! I love you...

The Spring of my soul! You are like a colorful flower of the blossoming trees... I love you with all the power of the awakening nature...

My busy bee! Before your call I was almost ready to send you a big bouquet of Forget-me-nots... Now I am sending you one huge dark rose... with the shape of my heart... for you to connect it with its stem - your love....... I love you...

When the clouds are dark, when your mood is as gloomy as today's weather, think about your constantly shining sun... - about me... and feel my warming rays from inside out... I love you!

Did you notice the sunshine outside today after all those rainy days? Didn't it remind you about the sun of your life that shines all-year-round emanating unconditional and endless love? Hope it did… I love you…
your Sun forever…

My ocean! Your waves of love make my soul feel like floating in a ferry of paradise… I love you…

Do you know when summer begins? And why summer is better than spring? It's spring every time you smile… and summer begins every time you hug me… and kiss me… whispering words of love… turning my heart into a hot-house… and my soul into a summer garden… under the burning sun… I love you my Summer!

My wonder! You are my exotic bird with the neck of a gracious swan, with the appearance of the bird of Juno, and with the magic voice of the meadowlark!
I love you my beauty!

❧❧

Weather forecast after 7 p.m. tonight… drizzle of light kisses until 8 p.m., then gradually increasing rain of hugs mixed with whispers of love, turning into a downpour of heavy kisses and extreme passion… I Love you…

❧❧

… Combine the scent of the flowers I sent, multiply it by one million, and even then it won't smell as attractive and desirable as you… I love you with one million roses in my heart…

❧❧

Wow! It's raining cats and dogs in Manhattan! And, by association, I remembered our first year in Brooklyn, when we had no car, and many times we were walking in the pouring rain under one umbrella, to or from the stores on 18th avenue and 60th streets… you holding my arm… seems so romantic after all these years… and so nostalgic… I love you… in the rain…

❧❧

Remember yesterday's bunny in our backyard?… You are like that little fluffy bunny for me… I want to take you into my arms and pet you all over… to make you feel cozy and loved… I love you!

When I am away and my eyes are open, I see your image
in pink and red... When my eyes are closed, I see your
image in violet and lavender... When I am near you,
I see you in shining golden yellow – the color of the
sun... I love you in all the shades of colors...

Listen to my heart... What does it tell you?... It doesn't
say anything... Because it can't... When the heart is in
the ocean of love, it cannot speak... it just sends invisible
waves of love, which can be intercepted only by the
person it loves... I love you in silent waves...

When you are angry, I feel like I chew an unripe bitter
almond... When you are sad or upset, I feel like I have a
huge piece of lemon in my mouth... When you are edgy,
I feel like I took a bite of a very hot pepper...When you
are smiling and happy, I feel like I am enjoying a
chocolate cake... Although I prefer the chocolate cake,
I like almond, lemon, and pepper too... I love you with
all your flavors...

⌒⌒

Earth holds us by its force of gravity… And love holds true lovers by its force of attraction… even if earth loses its force of gravity… I love you on earth and I will love you floating in 'no-gravity'…

⌒⌒

I told you it will rain!... and it's cold and wet… but I am fine with all the weather there is, as long as your smile is shining at me from behind the gloomy clouds, brightening the sky and warming my soul… I love you with shiny smiles of my own…

⌒⌒

Today in Manhattan the temperature is moderately cool, the sun is moderately warm, the wind is NW and moderately calm… only one thing is overwhelmingly and extremely hot and high today in Manhattan… my love to you… I love you with tropical heat…

⌒⌒

The challenge of the last few days is to find those 2-3 minutes to type my feelings of love. Which I did today… I love you with a power, which can be compared only to that of the sun felt in a foot's distance… burning and giving its energy without remainder…

Your symbol today is the flower... the one that attracts
the gaze and will not allow to look at anything else...
I love you with my undistracted gaze ON you...

The cold of the winter makes my heart warmer, as I look
forward to those wonderful evenings with you, when
we sit cuddled together in the coziness of our home and
looking into the white of the falling snow outside...
I love you...

Yesterday night the sky was very clear... and I counted
about two thousand stars... then I chose one of them as
your symbol... From now on, when you go to sleep
before me, I'll go out and try to find you in the night
sky... I love you... my never-fading star...

I am standing in the sun... enjoying the sun... my eyes
half closed... so that the open part looks at the sun...
and the closed part looks at your image, which is always
inside my mind and heart... I love you...

I love you rain or shine... or snow... or hail... or storm... or hurricane... or earthquake... or lightning...

...Spring is coming soon... to revive nature and to give more strength to our emotions and love to withstand the adversities of life... I love you...

When spring is outside... it is also inside... the spring of new hopes... the spring of enormous love and the spring of undivided devotion... I love you...

The bouquet of my heart consists of more flowers than nature has created... And each of the flowers contains a piece of my emotions for you... I give you all the love hidden in their wonderful arrangement...

The sun is shining... so is my face... to reflect the warm feeling of love to you... I love you with a BIG smile on my face...

I feel you in the rain… with each drop… with its tiny
vibrations… I love you…

Every Star is a Sun with its own Solar system… You are
my Star… with me in your System… I love you my
Sun…

Today I am sending you my love together with a pink
rose – the symbol of elegance, grace and gentleness. I
love you my grace…

I always feel circular waves in my heart, just like when
someone throws a pebble into a pond, except my heart-
waves are caused by my thoughts of you… I love you…

…Are you prepared for the snow storm? I am… We will
hug each other tenderly, and look out the window at the
beautiful white snowflakes… as a symbol of purity of
our emotions and love to each other… I love you with
each and every snowflake…

❧ THOUGHTS ON LOVE AND LIFE ☙

My love! When I wake up every morning, I thank God for giving me the chance to love and be loved one more day, to see and feel you one more day... And when I go to sleep, I pray for the chance of saying my morning prayer... I love you...

❧ ☙

Life is a short journey... and there is only one for each... Love is a journey of two... which is designed to make the journey longer... by feeling a second life inside and living for that life as well... the more we live for that second life, the longer the journey... I love you in the journey with you...

❧ ☙

Are you aware of the fact that the chance of finding your true love to become your life-long companion, who is from a place other than your town or school or college or work place, is 1 out of 3 billion? If you have, then evidently God MEANT it! I thank God... I love you!

Where there is love, there is peace. Where there is peace, there is kindness. Where there is kindness, there is acceptance. Where there is acceptance, there is understanding. Where there is understanding, there is harmony. Where there is harmony, there is love...
I love you in harmony...

According to the dictionary, Love has several antonyms, like hatred, dislike, despise, condemn, disdain, aversion, etc... It's so wrong... There should be only one antonym to Love... and that is Death... because once you truly Love... there is no point of return... it accompanies you until death... I love you until...

When you love, you give all of yourself... When you give all of yourself, the 'I' disappears... and when you try to find your 'I', you realize that it's inside the person you love... and then you love the 'We', where there is no distinction between 'I' and 'You'... I love 'Us'...

My mission in the short journey in this world is to love... Love without looking back... Love without regret... Love now... Love until the end of the journey... I love you!

My love! My heart! Our good future depends on the strength of our emotional and physical unity, on the best we can do for each other... I love you so-so much...

The miracle of love is the desire to make your loved one happy... I feel your love my baby and I am happy... And in return I send you all the red roses of my heart to cover you with my passionate and endless love...

The more I live, the more I realize that only the love of our loved ones will accompany us in the afterlife... I love you forever...

My love! We have to be strong in our love to each other
and be as one to withstand the turmoil ahead. Only Love
will protect us... I love you tenderly...
and passionately...

When there is love, there is the wish to make your loved
one happy... to devote all of yourself to your beloved...
I am all yours... now and forever... I love you...

My life! The power of true Love overrides the
unavoidable minor disturbances with the unfaltering
feeling of devotion and compassion... I love you
devotedly... and compassionately... and forever...

There is God who I love most, because God granted me
the chance to have you and Love you as much as God
loves us... which means I love you as much as I love
God... I love you...

With two more examples of famous people (Michael Jackson, Farrah Fawcett) gone – we agreed yesterday... life is too short... Too short to waste on comments that hurt your loved one's feelings, leading to arguments and mutual distress... We have to be focused on caring about each other's feelings all the time, not to say things that you would not like to hear from the other yourself... but to tell and do things that make your loved one happy... and remember... unlike life, which is short, my love to you is as long as the Milky Way... is strong as the diamond... is powerful as the lightning... and it strives to feel your love just as long, strong, and powerful as mine... I love you eternally...

Love, while you are loved... Love, while we are alive... Love, while we are not too old... Love, not to regret you didn't, if something happens... Love unconditionally... Love without counting – since Love is not math... The only calculation in our Love is (Your Name Here) + (Her Name Here) = Love... It always takes two to Love... And all it takes to Love is to give... your time, your emotions... all of yourself... I Love you in flames... burning down myself... until you see my ashes to believe, that no other man has ever loved his woman as much, and as devotedly and passionately, as I love you...

Our wedding was... like yesterday... and now we are
getting ready for our daughter's wedding... life is
short... and my heart longs for you even more to cherish
each second with you... and to forget how life is short
indeed... I love you...

I am in the bus, my thoughts drifting back and forth on a
dilemma... Is my love as big as the universe, or is the
universe as big as my love? I can't figure out which...
I love you...

Smile... It helps to relax... Tell yourself you are the
best... It helps to ignore those who are unpleasant... Tell
yourself you love your close ones more than yourself...
It helps to enjoy the most... I love you most...

The cats don't appreciate the grace of the flowers, they
will break them right in the middle... but even with half
of their stems gone the flowers try to keep their heads
afloat for the enjoyment of our eyes and hearts...
I love you...

Our strength is in unity... the unity is love...
love is strength... I love you...

Where love rules, there comes abundance, since love
Is abundance... I love you in abundance...

I am not sure who came up with the word love... but he
should have been a genius... to convey so much
attachment... so much wandering of the mind and
soul... so much happiness... so much devotion... so
much desire to merge with another person... so much
readiness to give everything... so much passion... just in
one word... I Love you!

Do you feel like a mother-in-law? I am trying to feel like
a father-in-law. And I can't believe it... It all seems so
fast... Today I was remembering our wedding...
and it seems like just one-blink-of-an-eye ago... and the
more I appreciate every moment with you... time is so
precious... I don't want to think of another blink...
I love you...

When two hearts are together, all misfortunes will go away… all the fortune will come… but only if indeed they are together… intertwined like vines… I love you…

∞WHEN SHE IS IN PAIN OR DISTRESS∞

My injured bird… I send you the best remedy in the
world – the balm of my everlasting love… apply as
much as your soul can take… it has no side effects…
I love you…

∞∞

My sweetie! Imagine my hands gently rubbing your
back, feel the pleasant tickling and the pain
disappearing… I love you…

∞∞

My love! Take my heart into your hands and give all
your worries to him… I love you…

∞∞

If only I could be the guardian angel of your dreams… I
would keep you in the world of uninterrupted love in
the Garden of Eden and let you wake up only when you
are completely refreshed and energized with the feeling
of happiness… I love you…

∽∽

I feel your pain... I feel your discomfort... I feel as if I
am hurt myself... and I want to hug you tenderly...
kiss all your wounds... and make them disappear...
or at least take some of the pain away... I love you
so much... breathlessly!

∽∽

Light of my eyes! I miss you so-so much... Do you feel a
little better now? Love forever...

∽∽

There is nothing worse than to feel the suffering of your
loved one... but there is the hope that the sincere prayer
and wish will help. I love you...

∽∽

... I pray for you and for your health... and send
all the warmth of my heart to you...
with love and compassion...

∽∽

My love, I suffer so much when I know you don't feel
well. It's worse than being sick myself. I send you all my
loving energy in the hope that it will make you feel
better... love you!

I hope everything is going ok? I want you to be calm and remember the priorities in life… your loved ones… all that counts… they are always with you… I love you!

⮸SHORT AND SWEET⮷

If I had wings, I would fly to you to give you just one kiss... I miss you too... and love you enormously!

⮸⮷

I did not find wings... and I do not need them... since my love will always reach you anywhere... anytime... forever...

⮸⮷

My love! Today I was day-dreaming and I saw you so close, so real... and as always so beautiful... I love you...

⮸⮷

I just called... to say I love you... and to say how much I care... and I am happy that, unlike Stevie Wonder, I can see the source of my inspiration... I love you...

⮸⮷

Let my smiling face and love-radiating heart be your companions day and night... I love you!

Giving my thanks on this pre-Thanksgiving Day for having you, your world and dreams in me, your love inside my heart, and your beauty in my eyes... I love you...

When you feel cold, just close your eyes and imagine touching my heart... it's always burning... with love... for you... I love you...

My soul... I looked in the mirror and saw your reflection instead of mine... I have completely lost myself in you... I love you...

My sweetie! Close your eyes and feel my passionate kiss on your lips! I miss you! LOVE YOU!

My everlasting LOVE! I need your voice and touch! Always love you!

My LOVE! I am thinking about you all the time! You are inside me! You are me!

My love! I have yet to give you so much love in this short life... I hope I have the time... I love you.

My love! If a million kisses are not enough, I'll add as many as you wish... I miss you and love you!

My half! I am counting the seconds to become complete by joining you! I LOVE YOU!

My love! My heart is calling you to join my feelings of love and admiration...

My everlasting love! You are my only one... always... you just continue to shine... I love you!

I love you more… and more… and to infinity…

Missing you and your voice… I'll call you soon.

My unfading fascination! Your love is inspiring… your touch desirable… your kisses unforgettable… I love you!

Ma belle! Your one loving glance and one caring word are worth a whole world! I love you!

My love! Even when I am busy as hell, your image is always in me… Love you…

My treasure chest! Each time I look at you, I find a new little surprise for my soul… I love you…

Baby! You are my unique Wife-Lover-Friend-In-One!
And I don't know which one I love more… I just love
the whole 'package'!.. Always… in joy… and in
sorrow… day and night…

No one in the world knows what is ahead… except me…
I know that ahead is my unfaltering love to you…
timeless… with no boundaries…

You are my oxygen mask! I won't survive even 5
minutes without you or without the thoughts of you…
I Love you!

L – Light is your symbol…

O – 'Opium' is your power…

V – Vibrant is your essence…

E – Eternity is your name…

LOVE you my life!

Strong is my heart… unaltered is my mind… firm is my
soul… with the everlasting feeling of Love to you… my
one and only… I love you!

…always thinking about you… with love and
tenderness… I love you…

My lovissimo! My beautissimo! My gorgissimo! I miss
you terriblissimo! I hug you fortissimo! I kiss you
tendrissimo! I love you enormissimo!

My love! After our mini-vacation it's so hard to be far
from you… All my thoughts and emotions are about
you… I love you…

The only thing that helps me to overcome frustrations
and depression is the thought of you… Your bright
image and the anticipation to see you soon… I love you!

Another Friday… another chance to be together
longer… to give each other the comfort… the smiles…
the love… I love you… looking forward…

On this sunny day today I am celebrating… one more
day with you… with you in my mind and heart… never
stopping the hope to do the same day after day… I love
you…

Very soon I will see you again – the flower of my eyes,
the remedy of my heart, and the essence of my life…
I love you…

Today there's no time to breathe… and yet my heart is
demanding to send its loving vibes to you… with the
wish to make you smile on this rainy day… I love you…

I hope this message finds you in a good mood…
to accept my love and kisses in reciprocation…
I love you…

My sunshine, my daylight, my delight
and my only desire... I love you...

My love! Long weekends seem even shorter than the
regular ones... And as usual they are not long enough
for me to give more of myself to you... my only one...
I love you...

My love... one of those 'no-time' days... with you in my
mind and in my heart always... I love you...

My Love! This is my Friday message to you full of lovely
emotions, passion and anticipation of a cozy and warm
Friday night... I love you...

Love you... Love you more... Love you even more...
and more... and forever...

… I just got out temporarily from the pressure of the workload to tell you how much I miss you and how much I love you, my chocolate cake…

… Very tired… but very enthusiastic… with all the love to you stirring inside… with the anticipation of seeing you soon… I love you…

My day is bright, my present is sunny, and my future is luminous… as long as all three are shared with you… I love you…

You are my water… my air… my food… It means without you I cannot survive… I love you…

Again Friday, another week behind… and as always looking forward to the magic of being together… so soothing, so comforting and so wonderful… I love you…

It's me… with arms wide spread… ready to lift you and swirl you around… to get you dizzy… just as I am from your love… I love you…

The world is meant to be a place of torture, except when we are together… I love you…

When you see a STOP sign, it's me… telling you to stop and feel the waves of love transmitted to you constantly from my heart… I love you…

My only one… mine in eternity… from morning till night my eyes seek your image… my heart seeks your presence… my soul seeks your aura… I love you…

It's unfair… that work sometimes 'steals' even those couple of minutes from sending a message to your loved one… I love you…

The good part is… I love you… The bad part is…
I suffer that I cannot share my love with you 24/7…
Love and kisses…

I am in love… and this seems to be incurable…
God has granted me the happiness of having this
lifelong disease… I love you…

My Kitten! I feel you curled on my chest purring
confessions of love and devotion in my ear. And in
return I tear open my heart to let you hear how it
whispers 'I LOVE YOU' with each heartbeat! Yours
eternally…

My little kitten! I embrace you and hold you curled up
on my chest to protect you from the cold… give you the
warmth… and feel yours in return! I Love you very
much!

My kitten! I need to stroke your fluffy fur and
hear your sweet purr… I love you…

My lovely kitten, I love you…
with lots of meowing…

My kitten! Too busy to be wordy…
just the short and sweet… I love you…

My pretty gal! You are my only mistress!... Victoria's Secret will never be able to offer anything to make you look better or more tempting than you already are! I love every inch of you!

∽∽

You are my endless lollipop... with the taste of an exotic fruit that does not exist in nature... and there is no other taste to compete... I love you with your unbeatable taste on my lips...

∽∽

Aliens have been reported to appear to people in the full disguise of the opposite spouse trying to seduce them... According to the reports, almost all husbands were easily seduced, except the ones with erectile problems... whereas none of the wives were seduced, until they figured out it was someone in disguise... I love you...

∽∽

My love, I want to see the 'beast' in you today... to feel the 'awe' of the waves and the power of unconcealed emotions and love... I love you...

If I were a sultan and had a harem of 100 women… all 100 of them would be the clones of the 'most loved wife' – (her name here)!.. I love you in 100s…

My cute bunny! I miss your eyes, your lips, your cheeks, your neck, your breasts, your tummy, your belly button, and everything further down… back and forth… I hug you in love… with love…

My beautiful naughty girl..! I am in an awfully aggressive-sexual mood! I need you and your shiny ..s right now… here… I long for you… with love and desire!

My fruit-cake with cherries on top! I want to eat you layer by layer, starting from the top and going all the way down until you are all in me… and I am ready to do this for breakfast, lunch and dinner… and one more time before going to sleep… I love you!

⤳⤳

I have a sh..load of work today, so I'll be very brief… I
want you now!… despite the sh..load, I feel you now!…
despite the distance… I love you always!… despite
anything!…

⤳⤳

My passion!… My love!… My desire!… I am looking at all
the half-naked women here in Manhattan… and the only
one I am dreaming about… is you… I want you and
only you… I Love you…

⤳⤳

My wish of the day: close my eyes, appear by magic next
to you on an uninhabited island, and… cover you with
kisses from head to toe… with my eyes closed… then
open my eyes and see the love in your eyes… I love you!

⤳⤳

Today I am ordering two quick kisses as appetizer, three
soft hugs as the salad, a long and slow love-making as
the main course, and more kisses for dessert… I love
you…

∞∞

My Lucifer is killing me today… He doesn't listen to any reason since early morning… I am embarrassed… Women are throwing smiley glances at the bulge on my tight jeans… If he continues harassing me, I'll have to come to you… ☺ … Save me… I love you!

∞∞

My love! I realized I have an incurable type of mania, called '(Her Name Here)-mania'… So you are 'stuck' to share the rest of your life with a person with a unique 'disease'… I love you as crazy as always…

∞∞

My (Her Name Here)Mania has transformed into Hyper(Her Name Here)Mania and Hyper(Her Name Here)Cannibalia… I am ready to chase you 24/7… and if I catch you, I am ready to eat you one small piece at a time… I Loveamania you…

∞∞

…We both started the new week a little sleepy… and the work, although in high volume, is of no help… Only the thoughts about you are keeping me awake… still feeling you… and wanting you all the time… and this keeps awake not only me… ☺ I love you…

My cutie pie I want to eat you, get ready. I love you...

With your flavor on my tongue... with your scent in my nose... with the feeling of the silk of your skin on me... and with me still feeling deep inside you... I love you...

I had a dream today... We were flying in a plane and we were the only passengers... First all stewardesses were serving us drinks and appetizers... then they were helping us to undress... and then they were all moaning when we were making love... and we were making love all the way until we 'landed'... into the ocean... and then we were making love in a yacht... I wonder when this dream will come true... I love you...

When it comes to making love with you, I like to be a Teddy Bear and a Grizzly bear at the same time... and sometimes also to be the Tiger, which I am... I love you like a pet... and I love you wild...

When I see you – it's a single shot… When I hug you –
it's a double shot… When I kiss you – it's a triple shot…
and when we make love – it's like a full bottle of
Armenian Cognac… I love you…

…unbelievably busy… with only one distraction (or
rather attraction) in my mind… you and your lovely
'muzzle'… I love you…

I want to be a tattoo on your thigh, or your back, or your
arm, or your butt… or to be a ring on your ear, or your
nipple, or your belly-button… just anything and
anywhere on you… so that I am always with you… I
love you…

Tonight I am going to bite your shiny ..s as a
punishment for not hearing from you ☺ .

But then I am thinking you might like it and stop calling
me, so that I do it every day! ☺

I love you… Lots of loving bites…

⌒THE JOURNEY OF LOVE FROM⌒ MONDAY THROUGH FRIDAY

Monday… my love is gently circulating inside, playing the tunes of soothing lullabies… and flying me on its wings to you… I love you…

⌒⌒

Tuesday… my love is sending messages of excitement… it wants to add engines to the wings to get to you earlier… I love you…

⌒⌒

Wednesday… my love is now rapidly moving… uncovering new sensations caused partially by the lightning speed of the flight… but mostly by the anticipation of feeling you in my arms soon… I love you…

⌒⌒

Thursday… my love… on its rapid flight to you… got into turbulence… and it stopped my heart… it won't start beating… until it feels the love back… I love you…

Friday… my love is getting ready to land on its target destination… to get lost in the maze of your burning emotions… in the tight grip of your love… I love you…

∞AUTHOR'S FAVORITE QUOTES∞ ABOUT LOVE BY OTHERS

"At the touch of love, everyone becomes a poet."
—Plato

"Love is a symbol of eternity. It wipes out all
sense of time, destroying all memory of a beginning
and all fear of an end."
—Unknown

"Love is the poetry of the senses."
—Honoré de Balzac

"In love the paradox occurs that two beings
become one and yet remain two."
—Erich Fromm

"A man is not where he lives, but where he loves."
—Latin Proverb

"You can give without loving,
but you can never love without giving."
—Unknown

"We are not the same persons this year as last;
nor are those we love. It is a happy chance if we,
changing, continue to love a changed person."
—W. Somerset Maugham

"If there is anything better than to
be loved, it is loving."
— Unknown

"For you see, each day I love you more.
Today more than yesterday and less than tomorrow."
— Rosemonde Gerard

"Immature love says: 'I love you because I need you.'
Mature love says: 'I need you because I love you.'"
— Erich Fromm

"Some love lasts a lifetime, true love lasts forever!"
— Unknown

"Love is not consolation. It is light."
— Friedrich Nietzsche

"The supreme happiness of life is the conviction
that we are loved - loved for ourselves,
or rather, loved in spite of ourselves."
— Victor Hugo

"Love would never be a promise of a
rose garden unless it is showered with light of faith,
water of sincerity and air of passion."
— Unknown

"Trip over love, you can get up.
Fall in love and you fall forever."
— Unknown

"You learn to like someone when you find out
what makes them laugh, but you can never truly love
someone until you find out what makes them cry."
—Unknown

"Love is my religion - I could die for it."
—John Keats

"Love is a canvas furnished by Nature
and embroidered by imagination."
—Voltaire

"Keep love in your heart.
A life without it is like a sunless garden when
the flowers are dead. The consciousness of loving
and being loved brings a warmth and a richness to
life that nothing else can bring."
—Oscar Wilde

"We are all born for love…
it is the principle of existence and its only end."
—Benjamin Disraeli

ABOUT THE AUTHOR

Armand Del Tor lives with his wife, son, daughter and son-in-law in Northern New Jersey, USA.

He has master degrees in Teaching and Psychology. He is a self-educated computer application developer and programmer analyst. Currently he works for one of the banks in New York City.

His major interests are World History, Psychology, World Literature and Music.

Armand Del Tor has survived two major catastrophes: an earthquake in 1988 and the World Trade Center Disaster on 9/11/2001. He is planning to publish books about these life-changing events in the future.

www.ingramcontent.com/pod-product-compliance
Lightning Source LLC
Chambersburg PA
CBHW030959090426
42737CB00007B/596